Hurricane Harvey

A Disaster Coloring Book

Written and Illustrated by:

Holly Cartier

Dedicated to:

Dad

Aunt Debbie

and

All the Survivors of Hurricane Harvey

Table of Contents

Hurricane Harvey first developed into a tropical storm on August 17, 2017. The next day it passed over the Windward Islands near Barbados and St Vincent causing flooding and wind damage. Harvey weakened in the East Caribbean, opening back up into a strong tropical wave before crossing the Yucatan Peninsula at Quintana Roo, with it came heavy rain and large surf. Once in the Bay of Campeche, Harvey quickly redeveloped in favorable conditions. Harvey became a Category 4 hurricane with winds over 130 mph before making landfall near Rockport, Texas on August 25th. Land quickly weakened the winds from the storm but the rain continued to fall heavily as Harvey meandered for over two days along the Texas coast. On August 28th the storm re-emerged into the Gulf of Mexico. Harvey then strengthened slightly while dumping more rain on the way to its last landfall in Louisiana on August 29th. Harvey moved slowly inland with its heavy rains, also causing flash flooding in Arkansas, Kentucky and Tennessee. It turned extra-tropical September 1st. Harvey completely dissipated September 2nd late in the day, while over Ohio.

Harvey took a heavy toll causing at least 91 deaths. The damage in dollars at first estimates ranks Harvey up with Hurricane Katrina as the costliest storms in United States history. Much of the extreme damage came from widespread flooding in the Houston metropolitan area, where over a half million cars were damaged. Across Texas approximately 13,000 people were rescued, 185,000 homes damaged with another 9,000 destroyed. Harvey directly impacted both the chemical and energy industry infrastructure, from flooding highly polluted sites to causing chemical plant explosions. 1.2 million cattle were affected with most having to seek higher ground from both ocean surge and inland flooding. Wind gusts of 132 mph were measured near Port Aransas. Heavy rain was widespread. The maximum amount measured was 64.58 inches in Nederland, Texas.

Though damage was catastrophic people pulled together in amazing ways to help their fellow beings. The outpouring of generosity began in Rockport near landfall with storm chasers pulling together to help one another shelter from the onslaught of Harvey. Neighbors and rescue personnel saved others from failing houses, nursing homes and shelters. With the ensuing flood, human chains to helicopters and every imaginable means to save others were deployed. Not just people got plucked from the water, many of their pets came along. Others made arrangement for livestock and went out in the flood herding them to higher ground. Even some wildlife were granted boat rides out of the flood or refuge in a house. The National Guard, Fire Rescue, safety officials and The Cajun Navy got others to safety as did neighbors with boats, jet skis and monster trucks.

ROCKETS
WXC

LUPE
ARKEMA
HAC '17

GAS

LUV CANE
TEXAS
HAC
17

BIG TRUK

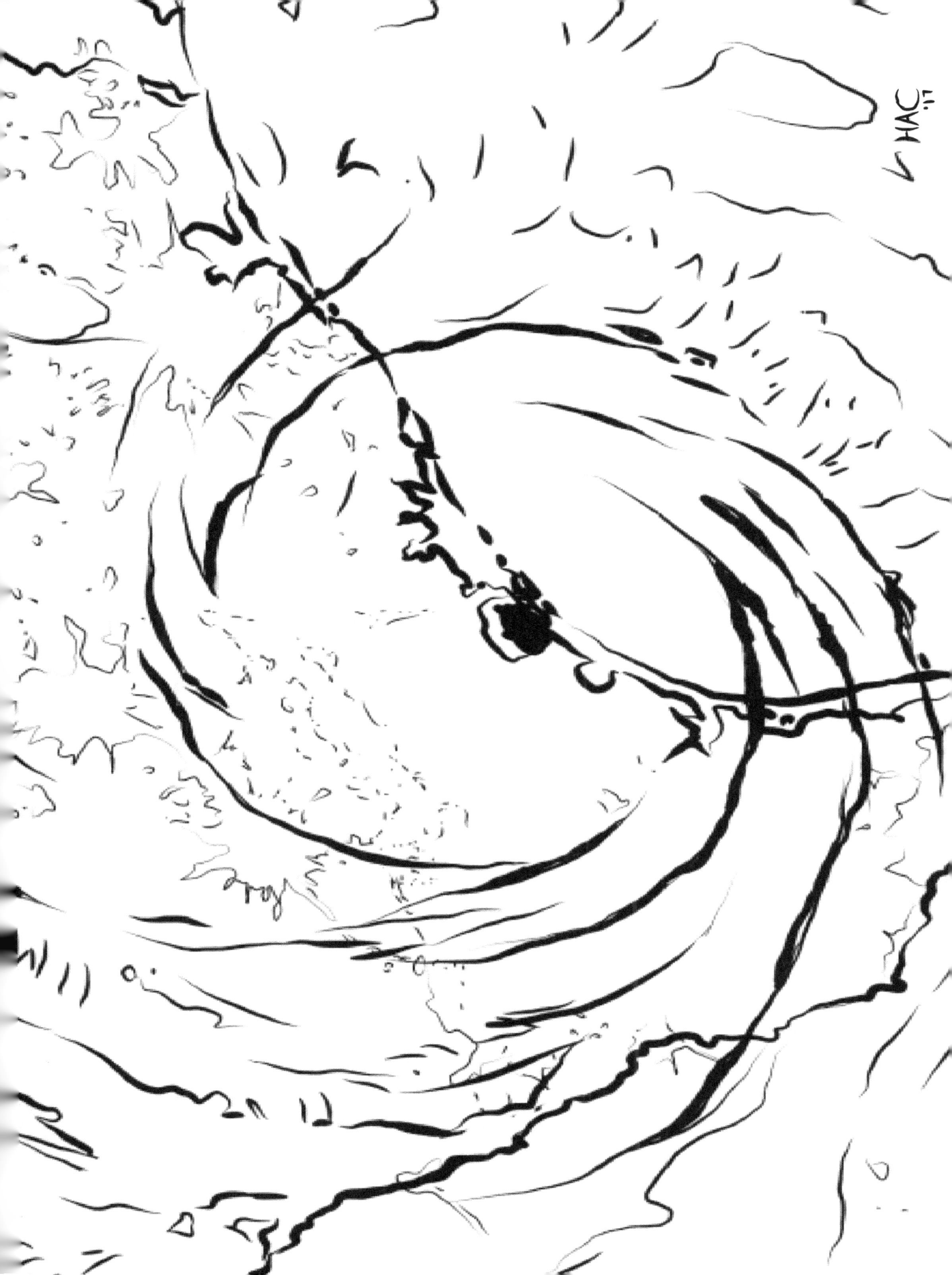

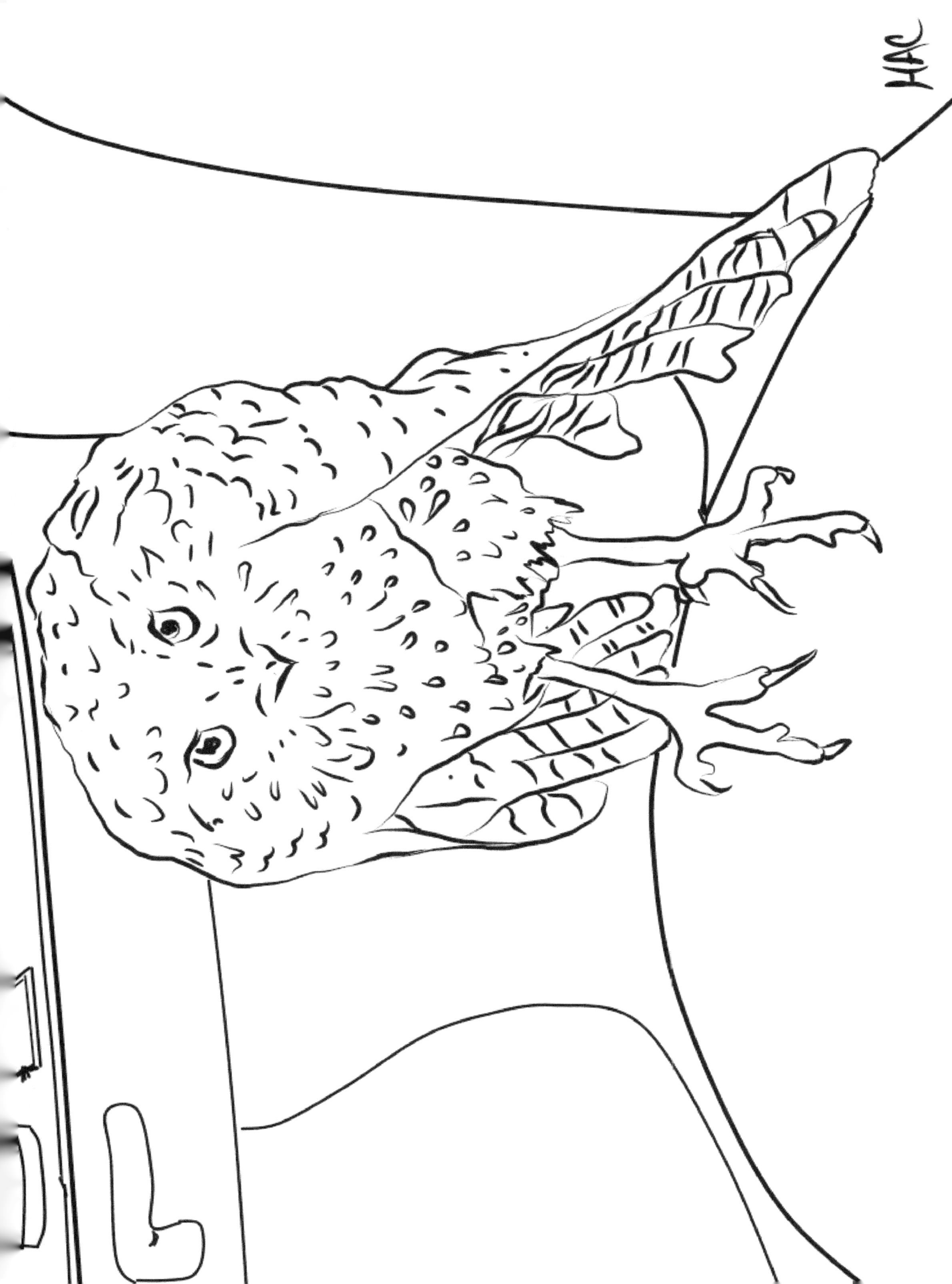

KHOU
HAC
17

SPEED
LIMIT
40

MEGA
LAKE
CHURCH
MEGA LAKE
CLOSED
DUE TO
INCLEMENT
WEATHER
HAC '17

TIDWILL LAKES BUY NOW
TIDWILL LAKE HOME SALE
LAKE
TIDWIL LAKE HOME SALE
2.19
2.25
2.15
MMC '17

HAC'17